Decorative Tiles

throughout the ages

Decorative Tiles
throughout the ages

HANS VAN LEMMEN

STUDIO

Frontispiece
A RANGE OF MINTON INLAID FLOOR TILES, MADE DURING THE 1860S FOR USE IN CHURCHES.
Top left: Pelican feeding her young with her own blood, which symbolizes Christ's sacrifice.
Top right: The hands, feet and heart of Christ, which symbolize his death on the cross.
Centre left: Date tile, suitable for commemorative panels in churches.
Centre right: The evangelist St Matthew.
Bottom left: Heraldic emblem of Lord Shrewsbury, specially designed for use on the floor in his church of St Giles,
Cheadle, built for him by A. W. N. Pugin.
Bottom right: Striking pseudo-medieval pattern.

Page 6
PACKARD & ORD HAND-PAINTED TILES, 1936-56
A fine set of hand-painted tiles made by Packard & Ord between 1936 and 1956. The firm of Packard & Ord was set
up by Sylvia Packard and Rosalind Ord in 1936. It was one of the few firms to make hand-painted tiles in the period 1930-60.
They were decorators only, employing up to thirty painters to hand decorate pre-fired blank tiles.
(private collection)

This edition published in 1997 by Studio
an imprint of Random House UK Ltd
20 Vauxhall Bridge Road
London SW1V 2SA

Text and layout copyright © 1997 Studio

The right of Hans van Lemmen to be identified as the author of the introduction to this work has been asserted
by him in accordance with the Copyright, Designs and Patents Act, 1988.

ISBN 1 85891 284 9

Designed by xheight design ltd
Printed and bound by Oriental Press, (Dubai)

CONTENTS

INTRODUCTION

During recent years there has been a growing interest in the study of decorative tiles, which can be counted amongst the most varied and widely found ceramic products. Although the history of ceramic tiles goes back to Egyptian, Assyrian and Islamic times, the first great flowering of decorative tile making in Europe began during the Middle Ages. The age of cathedral building in France, Germany and Britain brought with it the production of magnificent ornamental tiled floors made by specialist craftsmen.

In Britain, medieval tiles were produced in large numbers between the thirteenth and the sixteenth centuries. The earliest forms of medieval tiles are known as mosaic tiles; small, differently coloured geometrical pieces were put together to form larger units and patterns. The most interesting medieval tiles, however, are the inlaid tiles, so called because they were made by stamping a design into the clay and then filling the indentations with white liquid clay (slip). When the tiles were dry they were covered with a transparent lead glaze which after firing made the tile body look red-brown and the inlaid decoration honey coloured.

The designs on medieval tiles can vary greatly. They can be purely ornamental, with stylized floral motifs such as the fleur-de-lis, or they can be more figurative, with coats of arms, animals, knights on horseback or hunting scenes. A wide range of medieval tile design can still be appreciated at the Westminster Abbey Chapter House in London, where the inlaid floor tiles, which were laid *c*. 1255, have been remarkably well preserved.

Other decoration techniques were employed apart from inlay. Medieval tiles could be given a decorative relief surface with the aid of a moulded wooden stamp. In some rare cases the *sgraffito* process was used, as can be seen in the fine early fourteenth-century Tring tiles in the British Museum. Here the light coloured top layer has been cut away to reveal the red clay underneath so that the figures stand out against a red-brown background. With the Dissolution of the Monasteries at the beginning of the sixteenth century, much of the demand for inlaid tiles fell away and a new kind of painted tile from Southern Europe was introduced in Britain.

The Moorish occupation of Spain had transmitted the technique of tin glazed pottery from the Middle East to Southern Europe. When tin is added to a lead glaze it makes it opaque white, providing an excellent ground for painted decoration with ceramic colours. From Spain the technique was transmitted to Italy, where during the fifteenth century it became known as maiolica, the word being derived from Majorca, the island between Spain and Italy, which was a major trading centre for tin glazed pottery. The Italians made maiolica floor and wall tiles with ornamental and figurative decorations executed in blue, green, purple, orange and yellow. The fashion for these colourful tiles spread to Northern Europe at the beginning of the sixteenth century, when Italian potters began to emigrate to such places as Antwerp in Flanders, where they set up potteries.

One of these Italian potters was Guido di Savino who later changed his name to Guido Andries. He began to produce maiolica pottery and floor tiles which soon became very popular. These tiles produced in Antwerp even found their way to England, as can be seen at the Vyne Chapel in Sherborne St John near Basingstoke, Hampshire, where early sixteenth-century maiolica tiles were used to pave the chapel floor. The workshop of Guido Andries flourished; he passed on his trade to his sons and the pottery became a well-established family business.

At that time Spain ruled the Low Countries, and when the Dutch wanted independence, war broke out. Antwerp was sacked a number of times during the 1560s and 1570s. Artists and craftsmen fled from Antwerp to the relative safety of Holland settling in places such as Haarlem and Amsterdam. Here they passed on their skills and techniques to Dutch potters, and by the beginning of the seventeenth century potteries in Delft, Gouda, Utrecht, Rotterdam and as far north as Friesland in Harlingen and Makkum were producing what would become known as delftware tiles.

After the Dutch had won their independence from Spain, they became formidable sea traders. The prosperity of the Dutch middle class led to expanding towns where many new houses were built. There was money which could be spent on such luxuries as tiles, which made homes more hygienic and added colour and decoration to their interiors. Dutch tiles were also exported abroad and, because some of the better tiles manufactured in Delft were made for rich foreign clients for use in their palaces and castles, people outside Holland began to associate Dutch tiles with the town of Delft.

At first the Dutch produced tiles which were not very different from the Antwerp maiolica tiles, but around 1600 they switched from floor tiles to the production of wall tiles to be used in cellars, kitchens and fireplaces. These tiles were painted with characteristically Dutch designs, such as flower-pots, tulips and, later in the seventeenth century, ships, biblical scenes and landscapes. A decisive change also occurred around 1620-40 when, under the influence of imported blue-and-white Chinese porcelain, which was brought home by Dutch sea traders, the polychrome decoration on Dutch tiles (which showed its close links with Italian maiolica) changed to a predominant use of blue and white.

During the eighteenth century, the Dutch produced many tile panels. The potteries in Delft manufactured extravagantly painted panels with elaborately arranged flower vases as well as polychrome panels with Chinese style designs. In Rotterdam, Cornelis Boumeester painted large tile pictures with harbour scenes, seascapes and sea battles, while the Aelmis tile factory in Rotterdam produced panels with biblical scenes. These panels were often exported and can be found in such places as the Amalienburg Hunting Lodge (built 1734-9) at Nymphenburg, near Munich, and the Chateau de Rambouillet (built 1715-30) near Paris. The Delft potteries also undertook a prestige commission for the dairy at Hampton Court at the end of the seventeenth century; they made special large blue-and-white tiles, designed by Daniel Morot, the architect, who worked for William III, then king of both Holland and England.

The Dutch also travelled to Britain and set up potteries such as that of Jan Ariens van Hamme, who was granted permission to make delftware pottery and tiles in London in 1676. English potters soon learned the trade and delftware potteries began to develop in London, Bristol and Liverpool, which were to grow into major production centres during the eighteenth century. At first English delftware tiles were closely based on Dutch tiles, but by 1750 they had become much less dependent on them. English tiles at that time were sometimes executed in colours other than blue and white, and in Bristol potters developed the so-called *bianco-sopra-bianco* (white-on-white) technique which consisted of painting a pure white border decoration on the slightly bluish-white ground of the tile, creating subtle effects.

Another important development took place in 1756 in Liverpool, where John

Villeroy & Boch in Mettlach had a mass-production output similar to that of many English firms.

Tile catalogues of the late nineteenth century testify to the wealth of many decorative and figurative designs produced by in-house and freelance designers, like Walter Crane, who worked for Maw & Co., and J. Moyr Smith and William Wise, who worked for Minton. Apart from floral and patterned tiles, picture tile series became popular. Themes like the seasons and months of the year, and scenes from classical mythology, the Bible, Shakespeare, nursery rhymes and Aesop's *Fables* could now be found on tiles. New decoration techniques were developed or old methods were improved to obtain faster results, and it is not surprising that design quality and standards were sometimes sacrificed to meet increased production targets and greater profits.

A reaction to industrial design and machine production came in the form of the Arts and Crafts Movement, whose exponents, such as William Morris, Edward Burne-Jones and William De Morgan, were also concerned with the decoration of tiles. The establishment of the firm of Morris & Co. in 1862 was an important event. Here the workshop idea was revived with emphasis on well-designed hand-made products and the craftsman's pleasure in his own labour, as advocated by John Ruskin. Morris & Co. carried out a number of commissions for pictorial tile panels as well as individual tiles, painted in their own workshop on hand-made Dutch glazed tile blanks. This craft tradition of tile decoration was carried further by William De Morgan during the 1870s and 1880s, and his many hand-painted tiles with animals, flowers, ships and Persian motifs in glowing colours are now considered to be amongst the best products of Victorian tile making.

The vogue for Art Nouveau that swept through Europe at the end of the nineteenth and the beginning of the twentieth century had a considerable effect on tile design. The hallmarks of many floral Art Nouveau tiles are delicate, graceful and sinuous lines in combination with richly coloured glazes. They are produced as single tiles or as vertical panels for use in fireplaces, entrance porches and hallways, and many can still be admired *in situ* today.

The heyday of decorative tiles had largely run its course by the time of the First World War. An isolated attempt to carry on the crafts tradition established by Morris & Co. was made by the Omega Workshops founded by Roger Fry in 1913. Here some tiles were hand painted with avant-garde designs by Vanessa Bell and Duncan Grant, partly as an attempt to bridge the gap between modern painting and everyday design, but this venture came to an end in 1919. The reaction against excessive decoration during the 1920s and 1930s meant more use of plain tiles with mottled or egg-shell glazes. Some Art Deco tiles of the period showed imaginative use of geometrical form in combination with strong colours, while a modest output of picture tiles was maintained by firms like H. & R. Johnson, Richards Tile Co., Carter & Co., Dunsmore, and Packard & Ord, but nothing on the scale which had been seen during the Victorian and Edwardian periods.

After the Second World War there was relatively little decorative tile manufacture, the main production being plain tiles for everyday use. Tiles were hardly ever used for exterior decoration, as the drab concrete buildings of that period testify. On the bright side, there were some major avant-garde artists, like Picasso, Matisse, Miro and Salvador Dali, who on a few occasions turned their attention to tile design as an art form. The 1960s saw the increased use of screen printing as a means of tile decoration, but mainly for abstract designs and patterns.

Over the past twenty years, however, a remarkable revival of interest in decorative tiles has taken place. Victorian and Edwardian design has once more become respectable and many tile manufacturers have now begun the production of replica designs to satisfy an increasing demand. Architects and interior designers are again conscious of the value of tiles and are employing them more frequently for functional and decorative purposes. The refurbishment of many London Underground stations has included single tile design as well as tile murals by contemporary artists such as Alan Caiger-Smith, Maggie Angus Berkowitz and Jonathan Waights.

Now the computer is making an entry into tile design. Computers on which pictures can be drawn allow the designer to use simulated pencil and brush marks together with an assortment of different textured backgrounds. All manner of patterns and pictures can be created quickly and can be altered and amended at the touch of a button. The computer has speeded up the whole design process and therefore allows the artist to experiment with a greater range of options within a shorter space of time before a final selection of a particular tile design is made.

Although tile decoration has moved from the simple tools and methods used by the medieval craftsman to machine production and sophisticated means of computer-aided design, the hand of the tile designer guided by his or her own creativity still occupies a central place in the whole process. Its long history and the diverse range of techniques, both old and new, now available for the making and decorating of tiles, together with the continuing need for ceramic tiles of all kinds of functional and decorative purposes, has ensured a healthy future for this particular branch of decorative art.

HANS VAN LEMMEN
SCHOOL OF CULTURAL STUDIES
LEEDS METROPOLITAN UNIVERSITY

PLATE 1

MEDIEVAL INLAID FLOOR TILES, c. 1255

These tiles, showing heraldic lions with their tails intertwined, can still be seen on the floor at the Westminster Abbey Chapter House, London. Four tiles have to be put together before the full motif of the quatrefoil within a circle can be appreciated.

PLATE 2

MEDIEVAL *SGRAFFITO* TILES

Early fourteenth-century medieval tiles from Tring Church in Hertfordshire, showing scenes from the Apocryphal Gospels, about the childhood of Christ. The *sgraffito* technique here is unusual; the top layer of light-coloured clay has been cut away to reveal the figures against a red background. The scenes represent the following stories:

Top left: A man has been brought back to life by Jesus and is walking away, followed by Jesus and his mother.

Top right: Jesus is standing between two schoolmasters and two cripples; the latter will be healed by him.

Centre: Jesus straightens the broken beam of a plough.

Bottom: Jesus turns the water into wine at the wedding in Cana.

(Reproduced by courtesy of the Trustees of the British Museum)

PLATE 3

MAIOLICA TILE PANEL BY NICULOSO ITALIANO

Maiolica tile panel depicting the Visitation, which represents the biblical story of Mary, who, when she was expecting Christ, went to visit Elizabeth, who was expecting John the Baptist. It was painted and signed by the Italian tile decorator Niculoso Italiano (Francisco Niculoso Pisano), *c.* 1505, who worked in Seville, Spain. The Renaissance concern with central perspective can clearly be seen in the floor and in the ceiling which leads the eye to a distant view.

(Courtesy: Rijksmuseum, Amsterdam)

PLATE 4

DELFT TILE PANEL IN A CHINESE STYLE

Magnificent Chinese-style panel of Dutch tiles, manufactured in Delft during the second quarter of the eighteenth century and painted in high temperature colours. The influence of Chinese polychrome porcelain is clearly evident in the design and the colouring.

(Courtesy: Victoria & Albert Museum, London)

PLATE 5

DUTCH LANDSCAPE TILES

Late nineteenth-century panel, with Dutch landscape tiles with prominent polychrome Louis XIV borders; made by the Friesian firm of J. van Hulst in Harlingen. The colourful borders add a rich effect to the more conventional blue-and-white landscapes. These tiles were specially exported to Britain to be used as wall or fireplace tiles.

(private collection)

PLATE 6

A RANGE OF ENGLISH DELFTWARE TILES FROM DIFFERENT PRODUCTION CENTRES

Top: Two English delftware tiles with barred ox-head corners, showing St John the Baptist baptizing Christ in the River Jordan, and Moses in front of the burning bush, holding the staff that changed into a snake; Lambeth, London, *c.* 1725-50.

(private collection)

Centre: Two English delftware tiles with river scenes, within octagonal borders of manganese powdered grounds with Chinese-style quarter rosette corners; Bristol, 1725-50.

(private collection)

Bottom: Two English delftware tiles depicting harbour scenes, within octagonal Louis XV borders with buttercup corners; Liverpool, 1740-75.

(private collection)

PLATE 7

ENGLISH DELFTWARE TILES

Top left: English delftware tile depicting a vase of flowers painted in 'Fazackerly' colours; Liverpool, *c.* 1760.

Top right: On-glaze transfer-printed English delftware tile, showing a romantic pastoral scene within a rococo border, printed from a wood block and coloured in by hand; John Sadler, Liverpool, 1756.

Bottom left: English delftware tile with polychrome painted flower basket and a *bianco-sopra-bianco* border; Bristol, *c.* 1765.

Bottom right: On-glaze transfer-printed English delftware tile, depicting the Old Testament scene of the sacrifice of Isaac within an '88' border; Sadler & Green, Liverpool, 1761-70.

(private collection)

PLATE 8

CATALAN TILES, *c.* 1800

Two Spanish painted Catalan tiles depicting a ship in full sail and a basket maker, *c.* 1800. These colourful tiles are part of a distinguished tradition of Spanish tile making that goes back to the fourteenth century.

(private collection)

PLATE 9

FRENCH FAIENCE TILES

The French produced their own variety of delftware, which they called faience. Some important production centres for French faience tiles could be found in the Pas-de-Calais region, in such towns as Lille and Desvres and in the area around Beauvais, where small places such as Pouchon and St Paul had faience potteries.

Top left: Faience tile with stencilled polychrome decoration, made by Fourmaintraux, Desvres, Pas-de-Calais, second half of the nineteenth century.

Top right: Faience tile with painted and stencilled decoration. The blue has bled into the white tin glaze, producing an interesting effect; Pas-de-Calais, second half of the nineteenth century.

Bottom left: Faience tile painted in purple, with a shepherdess within an unusual decorative border; made in the Pas-de-Calais region, second half of the nineteenth century.

Bottom right: Faience tile with a striking painted and stencilled lozenge pattern; made by Ledoux, Pouchon, near Beauvais, nineteenth century.

(private collection)

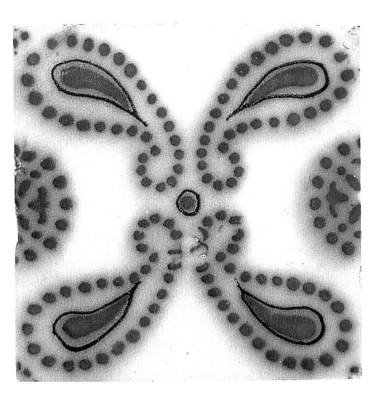

PLATE 10

BOULANGER ENCAUSTIC TILES

French encaustic tiles made by the firm of Boulanger, Auneuil, depicting the evangelist St Matthew. They are surrounded by tiles with French Gothic Revival motifs, and are on the wall of the entrance of the parish church at Auneuil, Beauvais, France; *c.* 1870.

PLATE 11

MINTON, HOLLINS & CO. MOULDED RELIEF TILES

Moulded relief tiles with translucent and opaque glazes, which were made specially for the grand staircase of the offices of the Minton, Hollins & Co. factory at Stoke-on-Trent. The letter H stands for Hollins, the owner. The tiles were put in when the factory was built in 1868-9.

PLATE 12

BLOCK PRINTED TILE DESIGNS FOR MINTON'S CHINA WORKS

A range of block printed tiles designed by the Gothic Revival architect, A. W. N. Pugin, for Minton during the late 1840s, but kept in production throughout the second half of the nineteenth century. The designs are creative interpretations of Gothic design, although based on thorough understanding and first-hand study of medieval pattern and ornament.

(private collection)

PLATE 13

MINTON'S CHINA WORKS BLOCK PRINTED TILES, *c.* 1880

Panel of six block printed tiles designed by J. Moyr Smith (signed IMS) for Minton's China Works, depicting scenes from a series of twelve designs illustrating Tennyson's *Idylls of the King*, *c.* 1880. Moyr Smith was a prolific Victorian designer who created many tile series for Minton's China Works and for Minton, Hollins & Co.

(private collection)

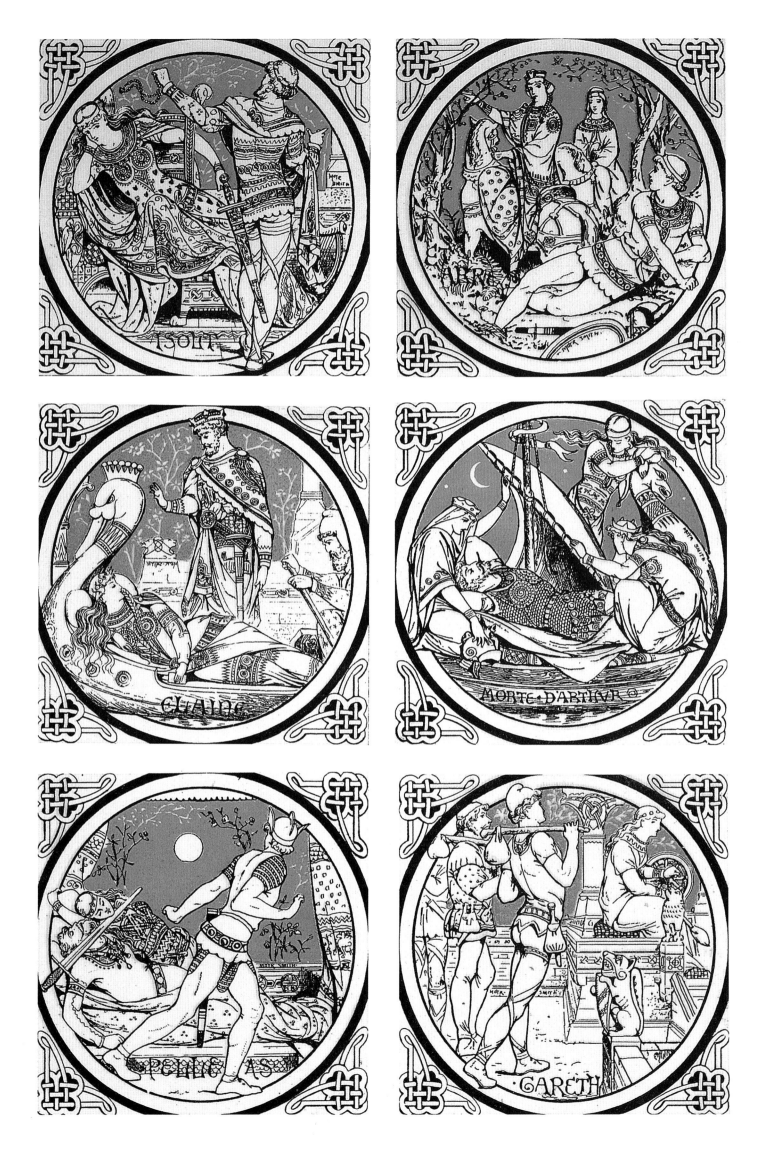

PLATE 14

MINTON'S CHINA WORKS TILE CATALOGUE, *c.* 1880

Page 8 of a Minton's China Works tile catalogue of *c.* 1880, with fine decorative and figurative printed wall tiles. Several of the tiles (nos. 1303, 416, 968, 508, 1063 and 995) are from the hand of the great Gothic Revival architect A. W. N. Pugin, who designed many tiles for the firm and who was a personal friend of Herbert Minton. Tile design no. 1303 at the top of the page, is a vase with lilies in the centre which is particularly interesting because this motif also appears in Pugin's book, *Floreated Ornament*, of 1849.

No. 1302, A.   No. 1302, B.   No. 1302, A.

No. 1303, G.   8in.

No. 1204, G. may work alternate with No. 1302, C.

8in. Tiles.

8in. Tile.

No. 416, G.   8in. Tiles.

No. 1324, G.   8in. Tiles.

No. 1323, G.   8in. Tiles.

No. 801, G.   6in. Tiles.

No. 950, G.   6in. Tiles.

No. 968, G.   6in. Tiles.

No. 1022, G.   8in. Tiles.

No. 508, G.   8in. Tiles.

No. 402, G.   8in.

No. 986, G.   8in. Tiles

No. 983, G.   7in. Tiles.

No. 1321, G.   8in. Tiles.

DOMINUS   PROVIDEBIT

No. 995, G.   7in. Tiles.

No. 1143, G.   8in. Tiles.

No. 1208, G.   8in. Tiles.

No. 1148, G.   8in. Tiles.

No. 781, G.   6in. Tiles.

No. 574, G.   6in. Tiles.

No. 612, G.   6in. Tiles.

No. 1063, G.   8in. Tiles.

No. 848, G.   8in Tiles.

No. 895, G.   8in. Tiles.

PLATE 15

MINTON'S CHINA WORKS TILE CATALOGUE, *c.* 1880

Page 37 of a Minton's China Works tile catalogue of *c.* 1880, with hand-painted scenes of little cherubs, birds, landscapes and townscapes. The three tiles at the top of the page, which show cherubs engaged in winter activities, were designed and painted by the artist Antonin Boullemier, who came over from France in 1872 to work for Minton.

No. S. 2172.

Panel 12×6.

No. S. 2173.

Panel 12×6.

No. S. 2177.

Panel 12×6.

No. S. 2180.

Panel 12×6.

No. S. 2180.

Panel 12×6.

No. S. 2179.

Panel 12×6.

No. S. 2178.

Panel 12×6.

No. S. 2179.

Panel 12×6.

No. S. 2173.

Panel 12×6.

No S. 2180.

Panel 12×6.

No. S. 2179.

Panel 12×6

PLATE 16

MAW & CO. TILE CATALOGUE, *c.* 1880

Page 42 of a Maw & Co. tile catalogue of *c.* 1880, with a good range of so-called maiolica wall tiles, which were moulded in relief and painted with opaque and translucent glazes. When seen in the right light conditions, such tiles create rich and opulent effects.

PLATE 17

MAW & CO. TILE CATALOGUE, *c.* 1880

Page 66 of Maw & Co. tile catalogue of *c.* 1880, with an extensive range of 6- and 8-inch picture tiles, most of which form part of larger series. The five picture tiles in the centre depict the seven ages of man (two not illustrated). The four tiles in the corners are part of a set of twelve tiles illustrating the signs of the zodiac. The three tiles in the centre at the top and bottom of the page show scenes from Aesop's *Fables* and are part of a set of twelve tiles. The four 8-inch tiles are part of a biblical series comprising twelve subjects. The remaining tiles are decorative and floral designs. Tile catalogue pages such as these are of great importance to design historians because they provide much visual information about the picture tile production of a particular firm.

2164. A, 35. 6 inch Tile.

2225. A, 4. 6 inch Tile.

THE OLD MAN & HIS ASS

2227. C, 7. 6 inch Tile.

THE GOOSE WHICH LAID GOLDEN EGGS

2229. A, 4. 6 inch Tile.

THE BOY WHO CRIED WOLF

2161. A, 31. 6 inch Tile.

2195.

2141. A, 36. 8 inch Tile.

THE GOOD SAMARITAN

2145. A, 35. 8 inch Tile.

THE LOST SHEEP

2051.

2238 6 inch Tile.

2138. A, 32. 6 inch Tile. †

5 THE JUSTICE

2237. 6 inch Tile.

2134. A, 36. 6 inch Tile. †

THE INFANT

2135. A, 4. 6 inch Tile. †

2 THE SCHOOLBOY

2136. A, 35. 6 inch Tile. †

3 THE LOVER

2242. 6 inch Tile.

2137. A, 31. 6 inch Tile. †

4 THE SOLDIER

2241. 6 inch Tile.

2144. C, 7. 8 inch Tile.

THE MARRIAGE FEAST

2148. A, 3. 8 inch Tile.

THE PHARISEE & PUBLICAN

2051. A.

2160. A, 30. 6 inch Tile.

2236. A, 4. 6 inch Tile.

THE COUNTRYMAN & THE SNAKE

2233. C, 7. 6 inch Tiles.

THE OLD MAN & HIS SONS

2230. A, 4. 6 inch Tile.

THE SWAN AMONG THE GEESE

2159. A, 34. 6 inch Tile.

A COMPANION PANEL OF RHODODENDRONS. No. 2194.

J. FLEMING & CO.

LITH., LEICESTER.

PLATE 18

SOCIÉTÉ ANONYME DES CARRELAGES CÉRAMIQUES DE PARAY-LE-MONIAL TILE CATALOGUE, 1911

Page 9 of the tile catalogue of the French firm Société Anonyme des Carrelages Céramiques de Paray-le-Monial, dated 1911. It shows four designs for pavements, with hexagonal inlaid tiles with borders consisting of square and rectangular tiles. The top two designs are particularly interesting because the motifs of the central floor area can be 'read' as three-sided cubes, creating a strong three-dimensional illusion. This type of floor decoration has been copied from Roman mosaic floors.

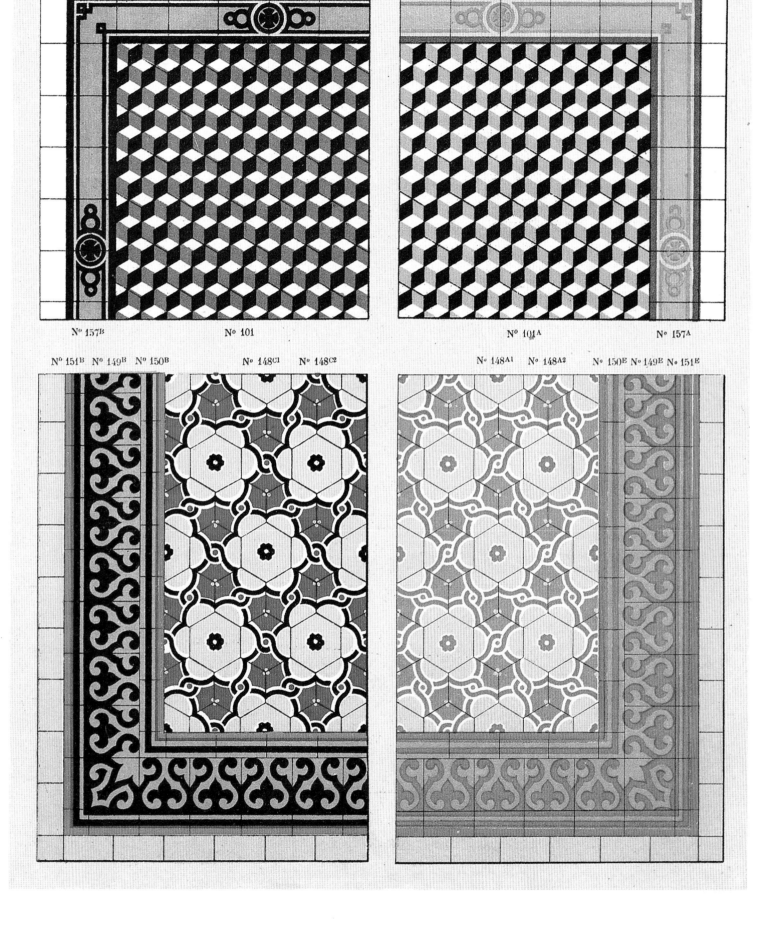

Nº 157ᴮ   Nº 101   Nº 101ᴬ   Nº 157ᴬ

Nº 151ᴮ   Nº 149ᴮ   Nº 150ᴮ   Nº 148ᶜ¹   Nº 148ᶜ²   Nº 148ᴬ¹   Nº 148ᴬ²   Nº 150ᴱ Nº 149ᴱ Nº 151ᴱ

PLATE 19

SOCIÉTÉ ANONYME DES CARRELAGES CÉRAMIQUES DE PARAY-LE-MONIAL TILE CATALOGUE, 1911

Page 46 of the tile catalogue of the French firm Société Anonyme des Carrelages Céramiques de Paray-le-Monial, dated 1911. It shows a large section of a well-designed decorative tiled floor. The central floor area consists of symmetrical patterns within alternating red and blue squares. The border has stylized and rounded interlocking plant stems and flowers with geometrical fret designs. The whole creates a rich visual effect.

PLATE 20

VICTORIAN WALL TILES, c. 1885

A set of six transfer-printed Victorian wall tiles of *c.* 1885. Such naturalistic flower tiles were popular and were used frequently in fireplaces of the period. It is important to note that the colour was added by hand between the black transfer-printed outlines, and the whole was covered with a transparent glaze for protection of the decoration as well as to give the tile an easily cleaned surface.

(private collection)

PLATE 21

TILE PANEL BY SIR EDWARD J. POYNTER

Panel representing summer, by Sir Edward J. Poynter, in the old grill-room (kitchen) at the Victoria & Albert Museum. The panel is part of a series showing the months and the seasons. It was designed in 1867-8 and executed in 1867-70 at the South Kensington Museum porcelain painting class by female students using Minton blanks. The classical design of this panel shows that Poynter had been influenced by Italian renaissance painting.

(Courtesy: Victoria & Albert Museum, London)

SVMMER

PLATE 22

ART NOUVEAU TILES 1900-10

Top left: Hand-painted tile with a disciplined design of stylized rose; *c*. 1905.

Top centre: Hand-slip-trailed tile with the areas between the raised lines filled with coloured glazes. Here a more naturalistic approach has been taken, but the sinuous lines of the stems reveal the Art Nouveau influence; *c*. 1900.

Top right: The lines of this tile have been pressed on to the surface with the aid of a mould in a tile press, simulating the technique of hand slip trailing. The approach to this design is much more abstract; *c*. 1905.

(private collection)

Bottom: A selection of machine-pressed Art Nouveau tiles of the period 1900-10. The designs consist of raised lines with colourful glazes added by hand to create startling colour effects. Such tiles would often be used in fireplaces of the period.

(private collection)

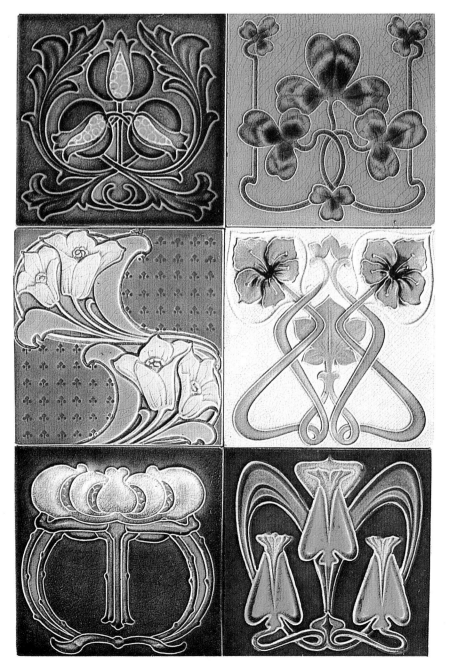

PLATE 23

DUNSMORE TILES, LATE 1920s-EARLY 1930s

A charming selection of printed and painted Dunsmore tiles of the late 1920s and early 1930s. The centre row is particularly interesting, with scenes from the *Alice in Wonderland* series depicting such well-known characters as the Knave of Hearts, the Walrus, the Carpenter, the Mad Hatter and Alice, the heroine of the story.

(private collection)

PLATE 24

MIKANA HAND-STENCILLED TILES AFTER DESIGNS BY SALVADOR DALI, 1964

Set of six hand-stencilled tiles produced by the Spanish firm of Mikana in 1964, after original designs made by the surrealist artist Salvador Dali in 1953-4 in Valencia. The tiles represent three pairs of basic themes.

Top: Life and death. Centre: War and peace. Bottom: Music and love. Dali has managed to give unique visual expressions to these basic themes common to all men. Death, for example has been symbolized by the image of a dead starfish on the beach, while war has been represented as four aggressive arrows closing in on the centre, seen against harsh and angular blue and white shapes. Each tile shows Dali's signature.

(private collection)

PLATE 25

'DINNER ON THE GRASS, CAMBRIDGE IN THE 50s' BY MAGGIE ANGUS BERKOWITZ, 1973

Tile panel by the artist Maggie Angus Berkowitz, entitled 'Dinner on the Grass, Cambridge in the 50s' and made in 1973. A fine example of modern tile design for use within an architectural setting by an artist who specializes in painting and firing glazes on clay tiles.

PLATE 26

COMPUTER DESIGNED
SCREEN-PRINTED TILES, 1988

A selection of computer designed screen-printed tiles produced by the Purbeck Decorative Tile Co., London, 1988. Contrary to what might be thought, computer technology allows for better custom-made design facilities and helps to offer an effective service in matching colours to complement decorative schemes.